Flip, Float, Fly

Seeds on the Move

by JoAnn Early Macken

illustrated by Pam Paparone

Holiday House / New York

For my mother, who has always
encouraged me to grow — J.E.M.

For Richard — P.P.

Holiday House would like to thank Amy Litt,
Director of Plant Genomics and Cullman Curator
at the New York Botanical Garden, for reviewing
this book for scientific accuracy.

Text copyright © 2008 by JoAnn Early Macken
Illustrations copyright © 2008 by Pam Paparone
All Rights Reserved
Printed and Bound in China
The text typeface is Joel 1.
The illustrations were done in acrylic paint.
www.holidayhouse.com
First Edition
1 3 5 7 9 10 8 6 4 2

Library of
Congress Cataloging-in-
Publication Data
Macken, JoAnn Early, 1953–
Flip, float, fly : seeds on the move /
by JoAnn Early Macken ;
illustrated by Pam Paparone. — 1st ed.
p. cm.
Includes bibliographical references.
ISBN 978-0-8234-2043-8 (hardcover)
1. Seeds—Dispersal—Juvenile literature.
I. Paparone, Pamela. II. Title.
QK929.M23 2008
581.4'67—dc22
2006037278

Take a breath and blow
on a fuzzy dandelion. *Whee!*
One puff sends seeds soaring.
Like small, soft feathers,
they parachute up in the sky.

Maple seeds whirl and twirl in a breeze.
FLIP, FLUTTER, *float*!
The wind lifts them up and off of the tree.
Away they fly like shiny green helicopters,
spinning and spinning.

Tumbleweed plants
grow as round as globes.
In autumn their stems snap off.
On the flat, open prairie, they ROLL, ROLL, ROLL,
sprinkling their seeds as they tumble.

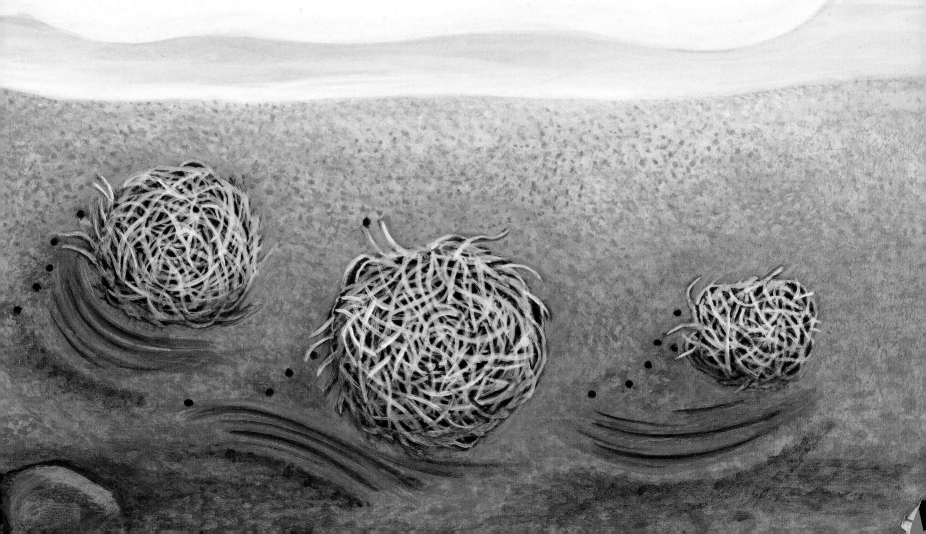

Basswood tree fruit clusters
twist in the wind.
Dangle and D A N C E!
In winter they drop.
Like sailboats, they glide
on the smooth, slick snow.

fruit

flower

Locust tree pods look like long, brown smiles.
They dry, split open, and curl apart.
Carrying seeds, each side scoots along,
sliding on slippery ice.
SKITTER and *skate*!
Seeds bump off along the way.

pod

seed

flower

Where water flows, it can carry seeds.
Even a raindrop can wash tiny seeds away.
Splash! SWISH! *Splatter!* SCATTER!

The air inside a coconut helps it float.
BOUNCE! *Plop!*
It drops into the ocean
and drifts away on the waves.

Some seeds move on their own.
Poke a touch-me-not seedpod in fall.
POP! *Fling!* The pod explodes.
The seeds are flung.

Surprise!

A wild oat seed

curls up in the sun like a comma.

The seed straightens out when it rains.

WIGGLE! *Jump!*

One way, then the other.

It works its way into the ground.

floret

fruit

spikelet

Animals move seeds around, too.
A bat finds a feast in a fig tree
and wings away with the seeds inside.
The seeds pass through its body unharmed
and fall to the ground in its droppings.

flower

fruit

A squirrel scurries
to gather up acorns
and bury them to eat later.
But does it use all the food it collects?
No! Lost acorns can grow
into strong, shady oak trees.

Burdock flower

seeds

Burdock seeds
stick to sleeves
and socks.
They cling to feathers and fur.
We carry them
as we hike
through the wilds
and drop them off
in new places.

People buy seeds
from garden shops.
Friends and neighbors
trade them and share.
Plants and seeds travel
on ships, trains, and airplanes.
Seeds on the move zoom over oceans,
across cities and countries,
around the world.

People plant seeds
in gardens and flowerpots.
They tend the seedlings and watch them grow.

Sprouts! Shoots! Leaves and roots!
Flowers bloom and new seeds form,
beginning the cycle again.

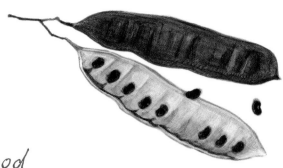

Seedpod
a fruit that holds many seeds, which are dispersed when the seedpod dries and splits open

Fruit
a part of a plant that
holds the seeds

Seed
the part of a plant that
can grow into a new plant

Shoot
new growth on
a plant

Sprout
young growth

Seedling
a young plant
grown from seed

Nut
a fruit or seed
with a hard shell

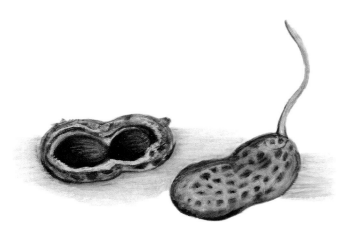

Flower
the part of a plant that
produces seeds. Most
flowers have brightly
colored petals.

Stem
the main stalk
or trunk of a plant.
A stem grows above the
ground. It supports leaves,
flowers, and fruit.

Leaves
the flat, thin plant parts that
grow from stems or twigs.
Most leaves are green.

Roots
the parts of plants that
grow underground. Roots
hold plants in place and
soak up water from the soil.

Apple seed

Tomato
seed

Impatiens
seed

Corn
seed

Notes

Many seeds cannot sprout where they form. Why not? Too many seedlings would crowd the same spot. Layers of leaves would block the light. New plants and old would all send out roots. Tangles of roots would compete for water.

How does a seed get from place to place? An animal, wind, or water might carry it. Or it might move on its own.

Many seeds end up in places where they cannot grow. A seed needs a home with the right light, soil, and amount of water. It may land in a spot with perfect conditions. Then it can sprout into a plant, grow, and make seeds of its own.

Sunflower
seed

Pea

Pumpkin
seed

Peach pit

Cherry pit